The Wonder of Words

A Parent's Guide For Raising Children Who Read

Curtis L. Ivery

Printed in the United States of America

ISBN 978-1-944068-87-5

Micro Publishing Media, Inc
PO Box 1522
Stockbridge, MA 01262
www.micropublishingmedia.com

Ordering Information:
Quantity sales, special discounts are available.
Contact the distributor Cardinal Publisher Group at
2402 Shadeland Ave A
Indianapolis, IN 46219
or call (317) 352-8200

Cover and interior designed by Larry Zelensky

To Sandra —

With much appreciation —

To my grandsons, Myles, Noah, and Mason,
and countless parents guiding their children
through the beguiling world of books.
May *The Wonder of Words* assist you
in igniting their passion for reading.

Table of Contents

The power of imagination is formidable – and grows only if it is fed early in our lives.

In childhood, we use our imagination to take us to faraway worlds, make the intangible felt, and make the impossible a reality. Our imagination allows us to expand our thinking, and with this, possibilities become infinite and endless.

Like any living thing, our imagination, and the curiosity it spurs, must be protected, nurtured, and continuously fed. Fostering a love of reading is the best way to feed the life of the mind. Dr. Ivery provides an insightful and eloquent analysis for making reading a part of the everyday life and culture of parents and children.

The poet William Blake once wrote to, "Hold Infinity in the palm of your hand." For Dr. Ivery, children can hold a book in their hands and see, as Blake also said, "a World in a Grain of Sand." Books can unlock the child's imagination and be the gateway to an infinite world, real or imagined.

The Wonder of Words is able to draw upon established models of literacy and explain them in ways that are accessible and directly applicable to the reality of children's lives – and to new ways of teaching that are transforming K-12 education. This book outlines practices to help guide parents and children on how to successfully incorporate reading with technology, something we increasingly face in the digital age.

Dr. Ivery focuses on key areas sure to inspire reading, improve educational outcomes, and nurture family relationships. He first focuses on the connections between reading and children's imaginations to open up new ways for kids to think about reading as an exciting activity they can share with each other.

For adults, Dr. Ivery links the importance of building a culture of reading with their children and how that relates with the challenges an educational system can present – so that the act of reading develops in organic response to advancing responsibilities and curriculum requirements the real world brings.

Foreword *cont.*

As Dr. Ivery highlights in the third chapter, according to the National Center for Education Statistics (NCES), children who are read to frequently from infancy are more likely to write their own names (50% vs. 40%) or read or pretend to read (77% vs. 57%) at an earlier age. The results of being read to are direct and immediate, and it gives children tools to succeed as they begin their educational path.

Dr. Ivery focuses on reading as an art that brings families together to create new family traditions. Reading helps to forge better relationships between parents and their kids through common understanding of what's relevant in their lives, ambitions, and challenges. To this point, he importantly discusses strategies of reading as they apply to the increasing significance of digital literacy and learning, including a focus on current and developing technologies. Through a Kindle or eBooks, parents can fuse their children's love of technology with the love of reading. In this way, reading becomes an essential part of their children's everyday lives.

Lastly, Dr. Ivery focuses on reading as the ultimate foundation of writing that is essential to academic achievement and instilling the confidence, if not dreams, of children in becoming authors.

Ultimately, Dr. Ivery writes about reading as intrinsic self-empowerment – the way that it gives reality to children's voices, ideas, and dreams, and allows them to imagine the difference and impact that they can make in the real world.

Those of us who admire Dr. Ivery know that his career as a nationally known thought leader, educator, author, and advocate for equity in education started in West Texas in his childhood home with his beloved library. Dr. Ivery truly loves the written word, but also has the passion for ideas, the impatient thread of curiosity, the critical thinking, and the intellectual blossoming that comes from it.

The Wonder of Words is Dr. Ivery's invitation to all of us to join him in his lifelong pursuit of knowledge, extending opportunities for growth to all. Accepting his invite is a true beginning to forging a future we all want for our children and our communities.

Joshua A. Bassett

Foreword no. 2

The year was 2001. The place: A summer arts festival on the edge of The Detroit River. It was warm outside, and I was strolling through the crowd, breathing in the fresh air and enjoying the sunshine. All around me, music was pumping. Hot dogs were roasting. People dressed in their favorite African attire were swaying past.

All in all, I was having a great day. Then something caught my eye. There, amidst the Kente cloth, handmade earrings and piles of shea butter, was a bookstore stacked with children's books. Immediately, I headed in that direction. Although I'd never seen a vendor peddling books at a festival, I thought it was a great idea.

I would soon discover how wrong I was. The minute I was within earshot of the bookshelves, I heard something I will never forget.

A small boy was clapping and pointing at a row of colorful paperbacks – early readers that sold for a mere $1.99 each. Excitement danced in his eyes and it was clear that he was thrilled. His mother, on the other hand, was not impressed. She grabbed his hand and led him away. A few minutes later, I saw the woman hovering near a jewelry stand, browsing through a showcase of beads.

My good mood was instantly dashed. I was shocked that a parent would deny their child a book. I was even more shocked when she pulled out her wallet and purchased a ring. After the woman and child were out of sight, I had a talk with the bookseller who confirmed that the scene I had just witnessed was not unusual. He had seen it occur with different parents and different children all day.

Now, don't get me wrong. I'm not implying that parents strolling through a festival should be on the lookout for educational materials for their children. However, I do recognize a problem when I see one. The child requested a book and the parent was the one who did not see the value. There is something peculiar about that picture, and I can't help but believe that some damage was done that day. Whenever I hear about young people either stumbling over words or not enjoying the process of reading, I reflect back on that experience. Why? Because everything begins at home, folks.

Foreword no. 2 *cont.*

Reading habits, like anything else, must be cultivated. For that reason, I rejoiced when Curtis Ivery told me about his intention to write a book that coaxed parents to be readers and detailed the many ways they can get their children to do the same.

Dr. Ivery is the ideal person to take on this task. He's an esteemed scholar and prolific author who has written on topics ranging from landmark Supreme Court rulings to criminal justice and urban affairs. He has also written an advice book for young men as well as a book on fatherhood and a series of middle-grade chapter books that promote family bonds. Clearly, he has a passion for reading and an understanding of what's required to build strong minds.

Using himself as an example, Ivery emphasizes the inspiration and ambition that bubble to the surface when a child develops a healthy relationship with books. After making that bold declaration, he then offers specific, step-by-step instructions that parents can use to convince their children that reading is, after all, an art.

His comprehensive list of strategies include family activities, unique outings, dinner-table discussions, literary role-playing, reward systems and more. According to Ivery, books should be a priority in every household and they should be introduced to children at every stage of their development – that includes infancy, the toddler and pre-school stages and beyond. His belief that children are never too old or too young to read is not a new theory. For years, childhood development experts and reading specialists have made this claim. Some have even cited studies that support the idea of reading to the fetus in the womb.

The advice offered by Dr. Ivery in *The Wonder of Words* isn't quite that extreme. However, it's pretty close. The book instructs parents to be focused, unrelenting and obsessive about vocabulary, daily reading exercises and well-stocked libraries in the home. Ivery, who relies on data and anecdotes to back up his premise, states that parents must lead by example.

Plenty of examples are presented on the pages that follow. Peruse them with an open mind and a positive attitude. They could help you and your children turn reading into a family hobby and a lifelong personal habit.

Ola Ivery

Introduction

Years ago, my daughter wrote me a letter thanking me for introducing her to a collection of books that she cherishes to this day. She was a bright child, outgoing at times, but quiet enough to settle down in her room and get lost in a sea of tales about faraway lands. When I noticed her interest, I was thrilled and made it a point to keep her stimulated. Later, after receiving her heartfelt letter, I realized that I was partially responsible for her literary passion. You see, as a parent, I had noticed a possibility. A potential.

According to my daughter, she didn't have a heightened penchant for reading early on. At the time, it was no more than a tiny spark in her mind. Sometimes she enjoyed easing into the pages of a book. Sometimes she didn't. I was the one who kept bombarding her with literature, the one who turned the spark into a raging flame and then kept that fire burning.

Until she wrote me, I had no idea. That's generally the way it works between parents and children. We see habits, interests, signs of talent or budding genius, and we nurture them. Or we see hints of laziness, a touch of restlessness, and we gently prod our children along a better path. In my daughter's case, I was the feather tickling something inside of her searching mind. She could have gone either way – a reader or a non-reader. She could have cast books aside or she could have plunged in feet first.

To my delight, she plunged in. To my surprise, she actually gives me credit. She says I nudged her. I say I was feeding a need. She says I cultivated that need by encouraging her and providing her with so much reading material she didn't want to let me down.

In the process of living up to my expectations, something took her under its spell. She calls that something, *The Wonder of Words*. My amazing daughter, Angela, says that wonder led her on a clandestine trip to a secret little nook inside her heart that is almost mystical. She has never returned from that nook and she is a better person because of it. She has mastered everything she set out to do and excelled in so many ways that any parent would burst with pride.

So, I dedicate this book to her. Meanwhile, I am also calling on other parents to follow that path I stumbled upon so many years ago. Find a good book and hand it to your children. Then find another, then another. The idea might seem far-fetched or even lofty, but it is not. It's a fundamental task. And it's a responsibility all parents should take very seriously.

Unfortunately, many think it's a job best left to the schools. I don't have data on how many parents read and how many of them enforce reading in their home. I'm not the word police. What I am is a scholar, educator, father and grandparent living in a high-tech society that is losing respect for the power and importance of those 26 letters we all memorized as children.

We forget that each book we pick up – no matter how long, comprehensive, or deep – is a compilation of that simple alphabet that is the pride and joy of all new readers; especially Kindergarteners. The random books we see on shelves, the newspapers we peruse, the gossip magazines that stare at us from grocery store check-out aisles, are all varying arrangements of those symbols we cherished at the age of five.

But something is awry, and I'd be remiss not to talk about it every chance I get. That something is this: We have transformed into a nation of nonreaders. Across the U.S., a collective scorn for books has led to a high rate of illiteracy and caused the reading prowess of our youth to plunge to a Third World level.

This raises other troubling questions: Is there a war on books? Is there a war on reading? As a nation, are we more interested in music, sports and fashion than we are in our capacity to comprehend the written word? Do we rely too much on video apps?

The shocking answer is yes. Reading struggles are real. In fact, they have become a critical concern in urban and some suburban schools. As recent as March 2019, the Skillman Foundation, Kresge Foundation, W.K. Kellogg Foundation and 313Reads – the Detroit brand for the national Campaign for Grade Level Reading, which is led by United Way for Southeastern Michigan and early childhood nonprofit Brilliant Detroit – began supporting and leading literacy-building efforts in the city.

Their mission is to meet a new state requirement for third-graders to read at grade level or be held back. This requirement comes on the heels of a 2017-18 M-STEP test of third-graders in Detroit showing that 15.7 percent were reading at grade level. Among the third-graders attending Detroit Public Schools, only 11.3 percent were reading at grade level while 21.2 percent of third-graders in Detroit charter schools were reading at grade level. Statewide, just over 44 percent of third-graders were proficient in reading.

I am personally familiar with Detroit, but in my opinion, this is a national crisis – and it's screaming for our attention. As parents, we must listen! We can't put all of the burden on teachers, babysitters, churches and task forces. We must step in and take personal control. No, we'll probably never be able to make a dog-eared paperback seem as exciting as the latest iPhone. But if we brainstorm, we can come up with ways to awaken childhood curiosity about what's going on inside the pages of at least one book. Try it. Do what I did. Place a book or two at your child's bedroom door on a weekly basis and watch as an eager fan of literature is born.

One day, those young bookworms may surprise you the same way my daughter did. They might write you a thank you letter for encouraging them to quiet their minds and read.

Curtis L. Ivery

Chapter 1

Unleash Their Imagination

Welcome to a world where anything is possible.

You can track the great migration of the wildebeest, learn all about the giant whale shark and peer inside the mouth of a raging, red-hot volcano. Or maybe you're more interested in historical and political figures – Thurgood Marshall or John F. Kennedy, perhaps? No problem. In this world, famous people – past and present – are as easy to locate as your next-door neighbor.

Where is this place of intrigue and how can you get there?

Look no further because you're holding it.

It's called a book.

Books are magical. They help children conquer fears, explore the world and pick up interesting fun facts. In the process of acquiring this new knowledge, children develop the skills they will need to grow into productive citizens, become effective communicators and achieve success in their chosen careers. According to the National Literacy Company (NLC), children who read consistently have greater reading comprehension and score higher on standardized tests. For children who shy away from books, the opposite is true. The NLC says the educational futures of up to 40 percent of American children are being hindered by their inability to read or a lack of reading. Further, more than $2 billion is spent each year on students who have failed a grade or have fallen behind due to poor reading skills.

This problem is compounded in overcrowded school districts with disadvantaged students. A survey by the National Center for Education Statistics (NCES) found that, in some communities, more than 60 percent of students in the fourth through sixth grades are reading below grade level.

What about your children? Are they reading well and are they reading often? If not, why not? In some cases, they haven't been exposed to other individuals who are taking the time to crack open a book. Possibly, the parent

> **66 Once you learn to read, you will be forever free. 99**
>
> - Frederick Douglass -

or guardian in their home struggles with minor reading challenges. In other cases, reading simply isn't stressed in the household and everyone (including mom and dad) is focused on TV, video games, movies and other technological distractions.

Chief among these culprits is the almighty video game in all its flashing action-packed glory. It offers such an endless array of fast-paced escapades and multi-dimensional quests that it's tough for books to compete.

As a result, books get a bad rap. Some children associate them with school and, therefore, feel like they're studying every time one is plopped into their hands. In their minds, books are work and video games are play.

But what if I told you there's a way to turn these attitudes upside down? What if I said that reading, like many things in life, is an acquired taste, as easy to develop as a love for apple pie? I know because I have a firsthand experience. I'm an educator whose thirst for reading was kindled at an early age. By the time I was eight years old, I was reading *Tom Sawyer*, the *Biography of Abraham Lincoln* and the *Bible*. When it came to the library, my appetite was voracious.

And it all started with my parents. Admittedly, I was a natural fan of the written word, a child with an eccentric habit of pulling out my dictionary every time I heard an unfamiliar noun or verb. But if my mom hadn't had a passion for storytelling, I honestly believe my love affair with language would have fizzled. It didn't because she strategically nourished my interests and kept me intrigued. Every night, she showered me with details about faraway lands that were more fascinating than the one in which I was living. After a while, I began to crave these adventures. They were my last chance to chat with my mom before bedtime and they were an opportunity to dream. And dream. And dream.

I was hooked and your children can be too. If you're a parent with a secret disdain for reading, chances are you need to sharpen your skills as well – which is something you and your child can do together. It doesn't matter if you're a consummate reader or a parent who hasn't read a book in years. You can shift your child's perception of books (and your own) in a few easy steps.

You are your child's first role model.

This means opening your mind and being willing to experiment with new approaches to parenting or dabbling in strategies you've never considered before. It might mean role-playing or wearing what might seem, to you, to be a ridiculous costume. Or it might mean allowing your daughter to imitate a storybook princess or letting your son sing like a pirate he once read about in school. Let's face it, your children are part of Generation Z and, frankly, they're known for being inquisitive, assertive and stubborn. They're precocious and they need lots of stimuli, cajoling and challenges. If you want them to adopt a new practice, you have to adopt one as well.

You have to do something unexpected and tinker with ideas you've never considered. Sort of like the TV families from the 1980's sitcoms. Some of the parents in those shows resorted to outrageously, zany strategies just to make a point to their children.

I'll never forget the extreme measures of one particularly creative couple. In an effort to teach their 13-year-old son about the realities of life, they moved all the furniture out of his room. Then the mom dressed up as a sales clerk and told him that if he wanted his bed and dresser back, he had to buy them from a fictitious store she called Furniture City.

It was all part of the laughs. Or was it? There are a number of television script writers (situational comedy writers included) who rely on the guidance of psychologists and other authorities to ensure their material imparts a positive message. So, while viewers tune in once a week seeking entertainment, they are also being informed or inspired to try something new.

Basically, that's the suggestion I'm offering now. Be ingenious, be wacky, if that's what it takes. Don't be afraid to be daring – even if that means donning the attire of some far-fetched character.

Experiment with outrageous plans and exciting household activities. Have fun with your family. And whatever you do, don't get uptight, angry or intimidated if you make a suggestion that falls flat. Or simply does not work. Everyone has experienced the awkward moment of expectation met with glazed eyes. If you begin with young children, you may be spared that eyes-rolled-back-in-the-head look for many years. But it will happen and you should not let it deter you.

 Too often, we ask our schools to be truant officers, our teachers to be truant officers, because we're giving them children who are not ready to learn. And if they're not ready to learn by the third grade, they know they're behind.

– General Colin Powell –

It's all part of the journey. Remember, you're trying to steal your youngsters' attention away from TV or videos and steer them toward resources that will spark their curiosity, teach them to be good spellers, improve their grammar and help them accomplish their goals.

You're not going to do that by doing what you've always done. You have to come out of the box and follow a new trail, one that will require a free spirit, a lot of resolve and some commitment. So don't be nervous about getting everyone in the family a new magazine subscription or pulling out the dictionary one night and challenging the family to come up with definitions of the words you happen to select. You are your child's first role model. A child who sees mom or dad celebrating books will be inspired to take this habit with him into adulthood.

But it all begins with you.

You are the one who must instill a sense of wonder for words.

You can do this by doling out reading assignments and being the enforcer who makes sure these demands are met. That means you might have to be the bad guy. You might have to call a time out on cell phone usage, stop purchasing so many video games and carefully monitor how often they watch TV. You might even cancel a few cable channels, or threaten to call off a trip to the movies. (Of course, you won't really do that, but ultimatums are powerful.)

I learned from one of the first books I read, *Tom Sawyer*, that there is power in doing something that looks so enjoyable that others, meaning your family, will want to follow suit. That is how Tom got his fence painted. He made it look like fun. There are so many great books for all ages and reading levels that you should have little difficulty finding something to excite your young reader at any stage or level.

Books will only survive in a house that welcomes them and doesn't allow them to sit unattended and covered with thick dust. But how do you do it? How do you establish and maintain a happy household of children who are just as eager about reading as they are about playing Xbox V?

Keep the faith and turn the page.

Chapter 2

Make Reading Cool Again

A good book is like an old castle on a hill. It might be tattered, maybe even abandoned. But when it's cracked open, something unexpected occurs. Winding stairs lead to a pirate's chest. A trap door is discovered. Dusty rooms are speckled with clues to an unsolved crime.

Just like the neglected fortress, a book can contain lots of surprises. Those surprises are the methods you, the parent, will rely on to convince your resistant elementary-school-through-high-school student to get lost in a sea of words. The methods can vary from week to week and from child to child.

For instance:

Pick an Animal of the Month – i.e., the Siberian tiger, the endangered white rhino or the fun-loving dolphin. Tell your children that the one who learns the most about one of these species will win a new video game or bike accessory. Or maybe he or she will get the largest ice cream sundae from their favorite fast food spot. Once a prize has been established, take them to the library and let them check out as many books as they'd like on the critter of their choice.

Make Reading Night Pizza Night – This works well because it builds positive associations. If every Wednesday night is the family's preferred evening for pizza, make that night the designated time for everyone (including mom and dad) to read for at least one hour. Do you think books will soon begin to seem as exciting as pizza? Not quite, but they will hold a bit more spark.

Read to Younger Siblings – If your child has a younger sibling or a pet, assign him or her the responsibility of reading them a bedtime story. The task will make the older child feel like the intelligent big brother or sister. They will feel more inspired to become better readers so they can show off to their kid brother. They'll also get a kick out of being the teacher for a day.

> 66 *Books are a uniquely portable magic.* 99
> - Stephen King -

Try a Costume Night – Once your children have launched their reading quest, come up with various activities to enhance their budding interests. Do they have a favorite character? Pick an evening for them to dress like the character, share stories about the character or even eat that character's favorite foods. For example, would your son like to be Harry Potter for the night? What about Bud from the popular children's book, *Bud Not Buddy?* Would your daughter get a kick out of sporting hair like the supernatural puffs worn by a young black girl in *Penny and the Magic Puffs*?

Host a Murder Mystery Night – Entice your children to read mysteries then set aside a night for cracking one of those mysteries. Or you can create your own. There are plenty of examples online of "whodunit" games. They're easy to play. Each family member is given a role that requires he or she to disappear at a certain time. Each time someone is missing, the others have to try to determine who's responsible for the abduction. As the game progresses, it will eventually end up with everyone missing and one perplexed family member trying to get to the bottom of the mystery. After playing this game once or twice, your children will delight in having the same experience inside of a book.

Be a Superhero – Plan a hero evening. Each child is required to read a picture or chapter book about one of his or her favorite heroes/heroines – Black Panther, Wonder Woman, Spider Man or one of the X-men or the Avengers. Heroes can also include top athletes and celebrities who demonstrate positive traits. For example, your children can read books about Serena Williams, Stephen Curry, LeBron James, etc. If they insist, let them read about a favorite rapper, as long as that person uses appropriate language, sets a good example and is not making headlines for bad behavior. At the end of the month, everyone involved (including the parents) shares a unique fact about his or her hero or heroine over dinner.

Trivia Night – Once a month or every other month, write questions on folded slips of paper and toss them in a basket. Each family member pulls out three questions to ask other family members about the book they are reading. For instance – what's your main character's name and why do you like him/her?

Invite a Favorite Local Hero to Dinner – Do your children admire anyone at your church, in your neighborhood or family? Ask them to drop by your home one evening and do one of four things:

- Share their love of books.
- Read a book to your children.
- Take turns with family members reading passages of a funny or inspiring book.
- Discuss books, talk about their favorite books or explain to your children why reading is essential. (This person could be the church's youth minister, a well-liked person who works at a nearby community center, an aunt, uncle or older cousin who is attending college or working on a job your children find impressive.)

Involve the Community – Talk to a teacher, community activist or minister about creating a neighborhood reading group. Adults have book clubs. You can start a book club for children with prizes.

Be Creative – Come up with your own ideas, chat with other parents and brainstorm.

If all else fails, try comic books. Also known as graphic novels, comics are a good way to get children to appreciate the power of stories on paper. It may not be what you have in mind, but it's a start that could help carve a path to the real thing. The bottom line is this: If reading isn't their cup of tea, you're not going to get anywhere by trying to force them to bury their heads in a historical novel or books about a situation they don't find appealing or amusing. Depending on the age of the child, you can start with picture books or early-reader chapter books. But no matter what grade, go for the books that are scary, funny or filled with activities.

Here's a few examples:

The Goosebump series	*Diary of a Wimpy Kid*
The Adventures of Captain Underpants	*Animals Should Definitely Not Wear Clothing*
Tales of a Fourth Grade Nothing	*A Bad Case of Stripes*
The Year of Billy Miller	*If You Give A Mouse An iPhone*

Are you convinced? Good.

Now all you have to do is convince your children.

> **A mind, once stretched by a new idea, never regains its original dimensions.**
>
> - Oliver Wendell Holmes -
> 19th century poet

Here's how:

- **Read with Your Child** – Make this an ongoing ritual. Have your child read passages from a book to you and you, in turn, can read passages to him or her.
- **Read in Front of Your Child** – It doesn't matter if it's a newspaper, a small book, a local, free magazine or an online article. Just read. Also, expand. Read something other than the *Bible* and the *TV Guide*.
- **Focus on Your Child's Personal Interests** – If all he or she cares about is sports, buy him a book about a boy (or girl) who is playing sports, trying to perfect their skill in sports or obsessed with sports.
- **Have a Treasure Hunt** – First, determine what books your children are reading. Then place questions about the books in strategic places around the house – behind the pillows on the sofa or under dining room chairs. When someone finds the question, he or she must answer it to get a prize.
- **Praise Celebrity Characters** – Point to favorite high-profile characters (especially those who appear on TV) who read or study to escape bad guys or solve complex problems – i.e., Spiderman is a college student, Batman has a huge library in his home and Doc McStuffins, the cartoon doctor to toys, surely must have studied carpentry. Or did she earn a degree in doll medicine?

Either way, you get the point. You probably have a few examples of your own. Discuss them over dinner.

Of course, you might encounter a backlash. If the minors in your home have made TV/video games and movies their chief source of entertainment, just the thought of a book is enough to make them breathe fire. Like any change, you have to stick with it. New traditions are hard to establish and old habits are even harder to break. You will have doubts. Your children will whine. And there will be evenings when no one will feel like doing anything.

Push yourself the same way you do when you're talking yourself into enrolling in a night class or working out at the gym. Get in the mood by visualizing positive outcomes. Picture your children winning a spelling bee, earning more A's on their report card or being awarded a scholarship to college. Realize that the more you invest in your children, the more they will achieve. Consider taking them to the library where they are a captive audience.

As the 19th century poet, Oliver Wendell Holmes, once said: "A mind, once stretched by a new idea, never regains its original dimensions."

Chapter 3

Build Mental Pathways

Readers are leaders.

That aphorism has been repeated more than any phrase I've heard in recent years. It's a succinct but impactful way of stating the obvious – reading can change a child's life. He/she becomes a dreamer. The imagination takes over and their innate creativity surfaces. Your child will feel inspired and empowered.

When that happens, he won't be as quick to shun the books you hand him. In fact, he'll request them. He'll get lost in them. He'll begin to think like a champion on a mission. Why? Reading creates new neural pathways in the brain and, eventually, these pathways (known as dendrites) join other pathways and form deeply rooted networks. The end result is confidence. Long-term goals. And determination. You have made a believer out of them and the changes in their brains are a natural consequence.

They include:

- Improved grades.
- An enhanced understanding of cause and effect.
- Critical thinking skills.
- A higher self-esteem.
- A vocation or specific career track.
- A longer attention span and greater concentration.
- Enhanced cognitive development.
- An interest in a wider array of extracurricular activities.
- Increased compassion and empathy.
- Improved analytical abilities.
- Strength, bravery and courage.
- Cultural pride.
- The ability to discern make-believe from reality.
- A love of learning.
- Greater curiosity.
- A desire to travel.

You'll get results whether your child is doing the reading or if the book is being read by you. According to the National Center for Education Statistics (NCES), a division of the U.S. Department of Education, it's important to start reading to your children at a young age. By the time children who have had this experience start school, they already have an upper hand and a head start. They have developed listening skills and learned to integrate sound with visual stimulation. And that's just the beginning.

> *Reading is to the mind what exercise is to the body.*
> - Joseph Addison -

- A wide variety of reading materials in the home results in higher student reading proficiency.
- Twenty-six percent of children whose parents read to them three or four times a week could recognize all letters of the alphabet compared to 14 percent of children who were read to less frequently or not at all.

Children who were read to frequently are also more likely to:

- Count to 20, or higher, than those who were not (60% vs. 44%)
- Write their own names (54% vs. 40%)
- Read or pretend to read (77% vs. 57%)
- Experience an increase in their IQs
- Reading to your child is a powerful bonding experience that will help bolster communication between parent and child for many years to come.

Things you may not know:

- The games you play with infants like "where's your nose" are the building blocks of language.
- You can introduce babies as young as six weeks to books.

There's an added bonus: Your children's inner book dragon is awakened. As they scurry to give it literary fuel, they might stumble upon heroic fantasies as well as the biographies and autobiographies of accomplished people. A number of real-life stories – Wilma Rudolph, Helen Keller, Booker T. Washington, Maya Angelou – provide inspiration for children, particularly those facing difficult circumstances. And then there's the imaginary victors – think Harry Potter, Oliver Twist and the savvy young Willimena in *Willimena Rules*. If the young readers can identify with any character – real or imagined – he or she will not feel so alone in whatever struggle they may face now or later in life. They will feel motivated to overcome their own challenges and reach for goals they once considered impossible.

All because of the role model tucked away inside of a book.

Create New Family Traditions

We've all heard it before – a family that prays together stays together. I'd like to alter that expression and take it a few steps further: A family that reads together reaches together. A family that reads together sprouts wings and flies. A family that reads together forms a tight bond, shares important information and has more meaningful discussions.

Meanwhile, every member of the family will strive to fulfill their potential.

The motivation lies in a shared desire to learn. Have you ever noticed that the youngest children in the family often follow in the footsteps of their older brothers and sisters? Contrary to popular belief, this pattern of success isn't totally due to genetics. True, heredity does play a part. But there's more to it than that. When one sibling sees another sibling studying, graduating from high school or pursuing a dream, she is inspired to do the same.

Success runs in families because parents who love books pass this love on to their children. The big brother watches dad flipping through a book. Then, little brother sees his big brother reading. Soon, everyone has adopted the same value system. Because of the family's mutual interest in reading, everyone – from the Kindergartener to parents – becomes a knowledge seeker who sets goals and aims high.

Since children are natural sponges, they respond to whatever is placed in front of them. If it's books, then so be it. They will cherish books. But you will have to make an effort to keep the passion alive. The best way to do that is to surround your children with books and turn reading into a family affair.

Here are a few basic suggestions:

Create a book-friendly environment – Start with the creation of a home library. This can be as simple as placing one bookcase filled with books in the family room or den. Next, purchase a small bookshelf for your children's bedrooms. If there's no space, position their books between bookends on nightstands or dresser tops. Make sure these spaces contain your children's favorite books. Include books he or she has read and/or books they plan to read.

> *So please, oh PLEASE, we beg, we pray, go throw your TV set away, and in its place you can install a lovely bookshelf on the wall.*
>
> - Roald Dahl -
> *Charlie and the Chocolate Factory*

Celebrate the hand-me-downs – I don't have to tell you what hand-me-downs are. In most families, the term carries bad connotations, mainly because it puts everyone in mind of the old jeans and t-shirts once worn by the older brother or sister who teased them. But when it comes to books, hand-me-downs are a different story. Literally. A hand-me-down might be an old copy of Dr. Seuss's *The Cat in the Hat*, the classic *Diary of Anne Frank* or *Amazing Grace*, an award-winning book about a spunky little black girl and her Nana. When one child finishes a book and progresses to the next grade level, don't discard it. Take it from her library and place it on the shelf of the younger sister. Unless they share rooms. In that case, leave it where it can be seen by both.

Honor their rite of passage – All families have some type of rite of passage. Whether it's your son learning to tie a tie or your daughter wearing her first pair of tiny heels, Rites of Passage Ceremonies are coming-of-age experiences that mark the beginning of something new and important and a shift from one stage of life to another. Graduating from picture books to chapter books is no exception. Make sure the family comes together to honor this significant achievement and more to come. For instance, the first library card.

Apply for library cards – To keep your child reading, he or she will need a regular flow of books. Keep it simple and affordable by getting everyone a library card. When one of your children signs up for his or her very first card, give the experience the attention it deserves. Everyone in the family should be present for this major undertaking. Afterwards, go out for ice cream or order a pizza and let the new library card owner say a few words about his first library book.

Post book-friendly images – Buy posters featuring popular children's books (either those they have read or a few you would like them to read) and hang them on their bedroom walls. You can also post them in a playroom, the kitchen and other sites around your home. The colorful posters will attract attention and remain in their awareness. The more they see it, the more they will absorb the message. Posters can be purchased at local bookstores, online stores and supply stores for teachers.

Go on book outings – Numerous family events revolve around reading, especially summer reading. Get online and look up events in your area or nearby communities. If you're going on a trip, take the family to a city that sponsors a book festival. I'm not saying you shouldn't take your children to water parks, playgrounds and beaches. By all means, do that, too. But, while you're at it, try to toss in a few reading events that stimulate the imagination and whet their appetite for books. Examples include the Virginia Reading Festival, Reading Rocks in Rockford,

Michigan, the Children's Reading Festival in Knoxville, the Reading Carnival at Wayne County Community College District (WCCCD) in Detroit and more. Most of the festivals include parades, face painting, scavenger hunts and other activities that combine reading with summer fun.

Declare a TV blackout – Some homes have a TV in every room. I know of a family with at least five television sets. That includes a 24-inch flat screen in the kitchen and an equally large flat screen in the bedroom of each of their children. If you're guilty of this, don't be offended by what I'm about to say next. I would like you to ask yourself what message you're sending to your child. Television is fine sometimes. It's entertaining; it provides escapism and it offers educational options like history documentaries, movies that end in moral lessons and picturesque shows about wildlife. Still, TV is not something that should be taken to the extreme. Balance your child's TV or video addiction by offering books as an occasional alternative. The best way to do this as a family is to have a TV Blackout night. That's right: No TV for an entire night. Instead, everyone in the family is instructed to focus on the book of their choice. Organize this evening anyway you please. You can hold it once a month or once a year. When it happens, be sure to have plenty of snacks and a few rules. For instance: video games and iPods should be put aside. During the reading period, everyone should retreat to their chosen spots and read to themselves individually. Or the family can come together and take turns reading out loud from one book.

If you must watch TV, then try this as a family project: Sit down together and watch the game show, "Jeopardy." How many questions can you answer? Were your answers correct? If you and your children have been reading on a regular basis, you'll be surprised at how much you know and how much more you enjoyed the program.

That's because reading is power. It also comes with some pretty cool bonuses:

- Reduced cable TV bills
- Spelling Bee championships
- Improved writing skills
- Expanded interest in the world
- Higher grades on report cards
- An advanced vocabulary
- Knowledge of other countries and cultures
- An impressive command of the language
- The ability to present persuasive arguments (verbally or on paper)

Whip out this list the next time your family insists they have better things to do than pick up a book. As Confucius said: "You must find time for reading, or surrender yourself to self-chosen ignorance."

> *"You must find time for reading, or surrender yourself to self-chosen ignorance."*
>
> – Confucius –

Make Room for Gadgets

It's a weekday evening and dinner is still on the kitchen stove, untouched. The dog is waiting to be walked. The cat is purring, demanding a neck rub. Several unopened books are scattered across the floor.

Meanwhile, two or three children are sitting alone in a silent room, staring down at hand-held screens. They're not interested in eating, exercising or reading. No doubt, their brains have been hijacked and stamped with the 21st century creed: Technology Rules.

With that in mind, a peek at a book might not be the first priority. Or the second. It's a contemporary conundrum that requires a contemporary solution. You have to approach your young readers-to-be with a flexible perspective and a resolve to meet them where they are: Rather than offering a dog-eared paperback, encourage them to download a book to the family's laptop, listen to a book or read it on a personal computerized device.

But first, listen to what they're talking about, so you can tune in to the trends they find important. Among first through fourth graders, an icky substance called Slime has been causing quite a clamor! Every kid wants it. So why not buy eBooks about slime (or something equally as annoying)? Don't worry, the fad will die out and their interests will mature. What will remain in its place is an unquenchable thirst for information.

By the same token, what if your preteen daughter is enamored with pop culture? Introduce her to the *Cheetah Girls*, books about a clique of teen fashionistas who travel the world, singing, dancing and shopping. Find out if she prefers listening to reading. In a year or two, she might switch, but in the meantime, let her do it her way.

That's the cardinal rule: Inquire about hot trends celebrated by your child and his or her peers, and use books as a secondary medium for these interests. As best-selling author James Patterson, puts it: "The fact is that our kids aren't reading books – or frankly, much of anything lately. Schools are underfunded, some schools even closing their libraries. Parents have to realize that it's their job, and not the school's job, to get kids into the habit."

> *"I find television very educating. Every time somebody turns on the set, I go into the other room and read a book."*
>
> - Groucho Marx -

By catering to their tastes, you are easing their resistance. A friend of mine with a ten-year-old son told me a story that fits this situation perfectly. She said her elderly aunt spent nearly three hours at the mall searching for the perfect birthday gift. After consulting with sales associates and going from store to store, she decided that her nephew (who's an honor roll student) would love the complete collection of J.K. Rowling's *Harry Potter*.

But when the "perfect" present was unwrapped, her nephew's reaction sent her mind into a tailspin. He stared at the books as if they were made of mud. Then he twisted his mouth into something that appeared to be a cross between a laugh and a scowl.

His aunt was upset…and confused. She exclaimed that when she was young, books were considered wonderful presents for a child of any age. (Probably not, but she insisted so who's going to argue with her?) Either way, she wasn't in touch with the three grave misconceptions shared by nearly everyone born in the era of iPhones, texting and Twitter. They are:

- Books are the worst present ever.
- If it's not animated, it's not interesting.
- Reading is for nerds.

By the time students reach middle school, the high-tech habit is entrenched. Many 21st century youth, even the ambitious ones, are captivated by things that flash, buzz and bombard their minds with whizzing images and blaring soundtracks. The nephew with an attitude might have smiled if his dear old aunt had brushed up on some of the latest electronic information gizmos. Here's an update on the latest ways to read a book.

Kindle – This popular electronic device appeals to children because it resembles a cell phone or hand-held video game. It lets them read by swiping pages and scrolling down a screen.

eBook – Children get a kick out of finding books online and doing what they enjoy most – downloading.

iBook – These are electronic books that are downloaded onto an iPad, iPhone, iPod touch or a Mac computer.

iPad – The iPad functions like a miniature laptop that's easy to carry around and allows the child access to the internet where he or she can access music, information and, yes, books.

iPod – Typically, the small, hand-held iPod is used to listen to music that is downloaded from the computer. But it's also a great device for iBooks and audio books.

Audio Book – While this might not be the ideal way to improve spelling and emphasize the importance of focusing on words on a page, it's a start.

Keep in mind there is only one thing children are drawn to more than technology. A challenge. Their young brains are in their formative stage, which explains why Lego building blocks are one of the top-selling toys of all time. Children like to multitask, be engaged, draw houses, create castles and connect dots. In the process, the brain's nerve cells (neurons) are activated and begin to communicate with one another via chemical messages from one neuron to another. This critical part of childhood development leads to cognition, motor control and more.

Parents can aid in this growth by fusing a love of gaming with a "like" of reading. As your children become more and more curious, you can light a smoking fire under them by assigning them responsibility for their own journey.

Here's how:

When you set up the bedroom bookcases mentioned earlier, make sure it's a hands-on experience for every child in your home. For instance, my grandsons made their own signs for their bookcases. They simply took a piece of construction paper and wrote the words: "Myles' Library" and another piece for "Mason's Library." This basic activity made them feel a part of the action in a way that is similar to being part of the action of a video game.

Video games involve the child. They participate fully and, in many cases, feel as if they are not only part of the game, but the creator of the game. Parents who understand the importance of interactive experiences can make the world of books just as enticing. There are a few suggestions listed below. If you implement them, remember, the goal is to get your child to feel as if he or she is playing a game, experimenting with strategies and manipulating positive outcomes.

Strategy One – Turn your child into a mini-researcher. When he asks questions or reveals an idea a friend may have shared (i.e., birds fly south for the winter), ask him to prove it. Tell him to Google it, check out a library book, look through his personal stash of books. Or he can order a new book online that supports the statement he made or answers the question he asked. After a few research efforts, your child will feel like a scholar and act like one too. He will begin searching for answers on his own and proudly reporting back to you.

Strategy Two – Once your children get the knack of researching and proving facts, the next step is to ask them to come up with their own theories based on what they might have read. For instance, they might be reading about Tom Sawyer's adventures and decided that his friend, Huckleberry Finn, is creating too much peer pressure. Maybe they'll come up with the theory that friends who don't go to school set a bad example for others. Their theories will require some critical thinking, but they will love the fact that you believe they are up to the task.

Strategy Three – Make it her responsibility to keep up with her collection of books. Ask her how many books she owns? Where are they located? Are they scattered all over her bedroom or are they stored in bookshelves or between bookends on her dresser? Are any of those books part of a series? Does she own the entire series? If the books are checked out of a library, when are they due?

Strategy Four – Depending on your child's age, allow them to observe as you place online orders for their paperback books, Kindle books and/or eBooks. After they read them, ask them to text you the titles with an emoji that fits the mood of their favorite character.

Strategy Five – Turn book night into a video game night. Ask each child to reimagine their book as an actual video game. How does the game work and what do the characters have to do to win?

Strategy Six – Recreate the technological sensation. Family members can act out the book as a play and use the same sound effects normally associated with video games. If explosive sounds or the roar of an airplane is needed, find them on YouTube and play the noises to enhance the experience. If the book involves food, place freshly baked cookies or French fries on the stove and let the aroma waft through the rooms of your home. Use your cell phone to find character voices or capture the fury of a raging storm. In other words, make it come alive.

Strategy Seven – Give your children books that take them on a journey or an adventure filled with absorbing activities and fun facts. Examples include Dr. Seuss's *Oh, The Places You'll Go* and *Where in the World is Carmen Sandiego?* (a book, game, movie and TV series).

The idea is to create action based on a book and make that action as exhilarating as an electronic game or adventure-packed TV show. The idea is to show that books can provide so much stimulation, the reader can get totally immersed in another world. We can't predict where technology will take us. If you, as a parent, can view these devices as ways of transmitting information, you can bring these perceived enemies over to your side. Stay on top of the apps your children are using and turn technology into a way for you to encourage literacy and knowledge.

You can be the best proponent of books in the world, but your children will likely disagree. When they do, ask them this question:

If video games are so superior, then why do the game creators choose to limit their children's access to them? According to Katharine Moana Birbalsingh, teacher, author and editor of *The Battle Hymn of the Tiger Teachers: The Michaela Way*, high-tech billionaires invent and market gadgets to children around the world, but go out of their way to prevent their offspring from being overexposed. As examples, she cites:

- The children of Microsoft co-founder Bill Gates do not have smartphones.
- Electronic devices are prohibited for students under age 11 at the Waldorf School in Silicon Valley that educates the children of the staff at Google, Apple, Uber and eBay.
- Facebook CEO Mark Zuckerberg's daughter is not allowed to use Messenger Kids (a free video chat app for children).

What are these children encouraged to do instead? **Read!**

View Life Through Your Child's Eyes

Let's call him Carl. At the age of seven, Carl could not figure out the words in his first-grade reader. He was a quiet, timid child who stayed to himself and spoke at the level of a four-year-old. But whenever his distraught mother visited the school, she was given the same answer: Carl would never be able to learn.

His mother refused to give up. She took him to specialist after specialist and finally tracked down a literacy expert who tested her son and offered hope:

He told her he was as smart as a whip, but he needed to hear lessons being taught. Every bit of information he took in had to be spoken out loud rather than handed to him as a lesson on a page.

Relieved, his mother enrolled Carl in a weekend support program that offered one-on-one educational training, ongoing assessments and comprehensive tutorials designed to address individual learning styles. Within six months, Carl's language skills had improved. He developed an interest in math. He devoured books on tape. He made the honor roll and, by the time he graduated from high school, had earned a four-year academic scholarship to a prestigious university. Carl, who now has an MBA, is a classic example of an audio learner. He has a unique way of acquiring information and his own personal style of processing it.

He is not alone.

Learning styles are as varied as jelly beans. We don't all think the same, laugh the same or dance to the same music. Neither do our children. So why would we put them in the same literacy box at school or at home? Do not make snap judgments about your children. Offer them choices and make sure you allow them to express their differences. Then, make sure you're paying attention. Does your child read every book you hand him but can't seem to explain what he just absorbed? When it's time to read, does your child procrastinate? Does he or she read very slowly or have difficulty sounding out words? Would your child rather go to sleep before bedtime, go to the dentist or wash the dishes than pick up a book?

> **"The whole world opened up to me when I learned to read."**
>
> - Mary McLeod Bethune -

Possibly, they are dealing with a not-so-obvious challenge. If reading is part of the issue, here's a few possible deterrents.

- Poor vision. Get their eyes checked to determine if they need glasses.
- Hearing loss. Hearing tests are a must for all children struggling with any subject.
- They are audio learners. Try a book, then a verbal lesson. Switch back and forth to see which method generates the best response.
- They are visual learners. Give your children audio and visual cues and notice how they react. Do they respond better to music than they do to images on TV?
- They have a reading impairment – Reading impairments run the gamut from dyslexia (where letters appear out of place or upside down) to alexia (neurological damage). Make an appointment with your child's school counselor to determine specific concerns and how they should be addressed.

Since all readers are not absorbing information in the same manner, don't select books based on your child's age. Select them based on his or her reading ability. It doesn't matter that a fifth grader is reading a book designated for a younger grade level. All that matters is that he or she is reading. The more they read, the more their skills will improve. Your job is to do all you can to encourage them and keep them on track. Praise them when they learn a new word or learn to pronounce an old one. Make a big deal out of any progress you see and, whatever you do, do not compare.

Never tell Boy X he is not reading as well as Boy Y, who might be the same age or younger. And do not push him to keep up with a peer who is excelling. The key is pacing and taking baby steps if necessary.

Readers of all ages enjoy the process only if they can go at their own pace. That's why it's important to encourage your children to read out loud as often as possible. Children love reading to other listeners. It gives them a sense of accomplishment and makes them feel more involved in the process.

Case in point: A parent I know once complained that her 10-year-old son simply would not read. As a result, he wasn't doing well in school. She tried everything: She bought him books, took him to the library and sat with him at night, demanding that he read. Nothing worked. Exasperated, she gave up. Then, a remarkable thing happened. She and her husband learned that they were about to have another child.

When the baby was born, the 10-year-old changed overnight. He became the proud, overprotective, bossy big brother and felt it was his responsibility to look after his younger sibling. He played with him, sang to him, helped him learn to walk.

As soon as the baby was old enough to listen, he also sat him down, pulled out his favorite picture books and happily flipped through the pages. His grades in reading shot up. By the time the baby was a toddler, the proud sibling was reading him bedtime story after bedtime story. In order to impress his brother, he was getting A's in reading himself. He also did something his parents had tried and failed to make happen – he started his own personal library.

The moral of the story can be boiled down to one word: Motivation. Your child has a reason, a point of excitement, an inspiration. Of course, I'm not urging mothers to have more babies or suggesting that all children will respond like this 10-year-old. But I am saying it is up to the parents to figure out what makes their child tick.

Observe them closely. Talk to their teachers. Figure out what buttons to push and discover the secret concerns flowing through their minds. In the process, exercise patience. While searching for the right tools, don't yell or criticize. Simply chat with other parents and exchange ideas. Just like Carl's mother, do everything within your power to build your child's confidence and create a reading environment that fits his other needs. One day, you will be pleased that you stuck it out.

And, by the way, so will your savvy young reader.

Chapter 7

Tell a Story, Then Read a Story

Can you repeat the word Mesopotamia ten times in five seconds? Probably not. Rapid-fire speech – especially when it involves a stream of rippling syllables – requires a lot of skill. That explains why so many of us trip on Mes-o-po-ta-mi-a. Or why the phrase, "Peter Piper Picked a Peck of Pickled Peppers," is often dubbed the grandmother of all tongue twisters.

But despite all the repetitive consonants, accomplished linguists can breeze through tough words and tricky expressions and make it look as easy as snapping two fingers. Likewise for certain pantomime artists and other performers. They blurt out ditties and riddles with the speed of a rocket. How? They practice, practice, practice. And they rely on a handy little technique.

The secret power of sound. In other words, they make it a habit to read out loud.

Skilled linguists perfect their craft by speaking words as opposed to skimming over them. The more they hear the words in question, the more comfortable they become with that particular pattern of syllables. They utter them aloud over and over – and they listen. After a while, they feel as if there is nothing they can't pronounce and no sentence they can't rattle off at an accelerated pace.

And so it is with your children's reading prowess. If a child has never encountered a specific word or heard that word spoken, he or she is more prone to stumble and be intimidated by it when it appears on the page of a book. He needs to hear a parent or teacher actually use that word. Remember all the hours you spent reading to your preschoolers? Well, you were building bridges and wallpapering their minds with a fantastic array of stories. Every night, they waited in anticipation for those make-believe worlds that sent their thoughts tumbling through an ocean of fantasies, images and ideas. Your kids loved it and so did you. Now ask yourself, why did it have to end?

Was it your idea to banish story time or was it your child's? Chances are, it was you. By the time a child is seven or eight, the average parent assumes the child prefers to read solo. After all, he or she is considered an adequate reader by then, someone with personal interests, favorite subjects and ongoing homework assignments. Of course, they want to read quietly to themselves. Wrong!

> **" I will defend the importance of bedtime stories with my last gasp. "**
>
> - J.K. Rowling -

According to Dr. Marie Carbo, founder and executive director of the National Reading Styles Institute, if a child is stumbling, go ahead and read to him or her. If a child wants you to do the reading, don't hesitate to step in and take the reins. As long as your children will allow it, read to them. Out loud.

Why? Children need to hear words before they confront them on the page of a book. If books are filled with words they cannot pronounce, they feel as if they are being tortured. But if those words are read to them, they respond the way one would respond to a familiar friend.

Dr. Carbo insists that a significant number of reading phobias are caused by limited vocabularies. Grappling with strange words is not joy! It's arduous work. The more exposure your children have to polysyllabic words, the less likely they are to feel threatened when they have to stare at them, sound them out and comprehend their meaning. Reading is only a pleasure when it's an easy and inviting task. But when it feels like a strenuous climb up a steep mountain, it's a slow form of torment.

That's why bedtime stories are so unforgettable. Your children hear them while spending quality time with you, exploring new vistas and learning in the process. Each new word they hear is a jewel that lights up their minds and preps them for their own reading conquest. Everyday words like "Complicated," "Removal," and "Hovering" become warm and fuzzy friends – fun and easy to embrace. And the new words that happen along their reading path – terms like "Savvy," "Subtle," and "Obscure" – are exciting opportunities to repeat something heard the previous week.

If you'd like to take it further, you can make vocabulary-building exercises part of the family routine. During your weekly story hour, ask your children to jot down at least one new word they learned while reading that evening. Next, instruct them to look it up in the dictionary, write it down and/or share the meaning with you and their siblings.

A Word of Caution: Be gentle and flexible. If you're boosting vocabulary, have a plan, not an attack mission. Make sure the words you're sharing are terms you noticed in your child's reader or library book, and be sure to sprinkle them lightly throughout your conversations – during dinner or a drive to the park. Don't overdo it and don't adhere to uncompromising standards. If your eighth grader is reading at a sixth-grade level, allow him or her to go with the flow. Introduce words based on your child's development and not the guidelines imposed by educators. Take them at their own pace and applaud when they begin showing off their mastery of vocabulary that may have been foreign to them weeks earlier.

Your children are flowers budding in their own way and basking in the experiences of their choice. If you want them to view reading as paradise, allow them to romp in the tales that match their development, not their age. Turn your family's evenings into word landscapes that encourage your children to show off their new knowledge. Indulge in board games that celebrate word power – Scrabble, Bobble, Pictionary, Upwords and Alfapet. Or look for online digital word challenges that allow everyone to join in the fun.

Throughout it all, don't forget the number one wordsmith strategy! **Read Out Loud!**

For further enrichment, here are a few vocabulary words to consider.

Ages 7-8	**Ages 9-10**	Satisfaction	Horrendous	Benevolent
Abundant	Affordable	Screech	Immortal	Blissful
Around	Atmosphere	Solidify	Magnificent	Contestant
Basic	Championship	Successful	Majestic	Credulous
Before	Chute	Toil	Outrageous	Crestfallen
Boastful	Destiny	Tomorrow	Plentiful	Dispense
Brilliant	Explode	Twinkled	Presentable	Exploitation
Capture	Freight	Unconventional	Remarkable	Lethargic
Continue	Furniture	Windowsill	Scour	Magnanimous
Gallop	Genius		Solitude	Malevolent
Gentle	Genuine	**Ages 11-13**	Temptation	Miraculous
Gigantic	Glorified	Ambitious	Treasure	Preposterous
Glory	Gracious	Arguably		Scintillating
Hundred	Jubilant	Brutality		Tumultuous
Incredible	Measles	Clarification	**Ages 14**	Tyrant
Opportunity	Mighty	Compassion	**and Up**	Vehemently
Recognize	Mystical	Consequence	Adversary	Zealous
Scold	Paradise	Delirious	Amiable	
Serious	Patience	Enthusiastic	Appease	
Terrified	Pierce	Generous	Artifact	
Wonder	Position	Gregarious	Audacity	
			Avarice	

Chapter 8

Turn Them Into Authors

It was the end of a long day and all I wanted to do was chat with my grandson. When I couldn't reach him by calling, I sent a text and relaxed, knowing he would be pleased to hear from me. But when I glanced down at my cell phone, I was a bit taken aback.

There, in bold type were the letters IMU, followed by a bright yellow row of smiley-faced emojis. One was waving and the others were flashing big, goofy smiles.

At first, I laughed. Then, after a long pause, I sighed.

I began to worry about literacy among young people and I began to connect some of their challenges to their dependency on text messaging. So many youths rely on texting that they neglect full sentences and don't feel the need to spell out entire words. As I stared at my grandson's letters standing alone without a message, I began to fret that, perhaps, our children were losing the ability to communicate. And I couldn't help but wonder about the role books would play in their future. I shuddered at the thought that scanning text messages was their idea of reading.

When I texted my response to my grandson's text, I inserted big words in a long paragraph that included perfect punctuation. It was my way of making sure he doesn't forget that a text message is not an excuse for improper syntax and poor grammar.

But the experience was a wake-up call. It forced me to face the fact that texting and all of its absurd abbreviations is here to stay. "IDK" (I don't know), "LOL" (laugh out loud) and "BRB" (be right back) are now an established lingo that has become a popular form of communication. Unfortunately, this expanding list of acronyms is threatening to weaken the language and destroy the fundamentals of reading and writing.

I believe the text messaging habit has the potential to turn our children into lazy readers and even worse spellers. That's a predictable consequence of a microwave society with an emphasis on instant gratification. But I'm not ready to fast forward to doomsday thinking. There's hope. Texting is fun, quick and easy, but there is at least one old school habit that should make your children sit up and take notice.

> *The more that you read, the more things you will know. The more that you learn, the more places you'll go.*
>
> - Dr. Seuss -

They can write a book.

I know that sounds like a blast out of left field, but it makes perfect sense. Drastic situations require drastic reactions. And what could be more drastic for this I-want-it-now generation than the discipline of becoming an author?

Authorship is a journey that requires focus and forces the writer to process thoughts. It's an ideal way for young minds to develop, contemplate and ponder. It teaches youth that everything doesn't happen overnight. It instills a sense of commitment and stick-to-itiveness and leads them down the road to a unique academic achievement. The result is pride, purpose and accomplishment. They have joined an unusual tribe – a pen-wielding group of children who have done something the average adult has not tackled.

Child authors, just like child entrepreneurs, are a growing trend. Not only are children writing books, they are self-publishing them and/or getting them printed on demand by Amazon. In fact, there are community programs that walk them through the step-by-step process of getting their words on paper and turning them into a product that can be marketed and sold.

The premise is that if they can write a book, they will read a book. One act will bolster the other. Years ago, Southfield, Michigan, was the site of an innovative workshop dubbed, "Look, Mom, I'm An Author." For a fee, children attended sessions that guided them as they conjured up ideas and jotted them down on paper. Instructors assisted with the wording and helped them structure their content. Afterwards, they were led through self-editing sessions that prepped their short picture books for printing. Next came the sheer excitement of holding their own works – replete with glossy cover and crisp, illustrated pages – in their very own hands.

Although this program no longer exists, summer camps, afterschool sessions and Saturday workshops are being held at churches, activity centers and schools across the country. There are also online programs that can turn a child as young as eight years old into a budding author. By following the instructions on the internet site, parents can create a family book-writing project at home.

The book produced will become a treasure – in your child's eyes and your own. It also will be part of the library they've been building. Your young author's eyes will light up when she notices her book on a shelf, when you post it on Facebook or she sees her creation on Amazon, right along with books by Christopher Paul Curtis and J.K. Rowling.

Don't dismiss creating a book with your young child the old-fashioned way. Children enjoy crafts and it is a way to get them unplugged. You can purchase colored paper, drawing paper and some markers. Staple the paper with a colored paper cover and have your child write and illustrate a story. You can decorate the book with ribbon or stickers. It is the idea of encouraging creativity. You can show your child the different parts of a book and discuss them. How does the book begin? How does it end? Stay engaged according to your child's interests. And let them make a mess. Sometimes, it is the parent who prefers the electronic babysitter. After all, there are no stains to clean up. We can look at our own smartphone while our child is likewise engaged. We need to unplug as well.

But the journey doesn't stop there. If your goal is to combat high-tech dependency and fight off the doldrums caused by too much texting, you have to continue to come up with new ideas and seek out new programs. The National Reading Foundation offers an innovative afterschool reading program that operates in New York, Detroit, Los Angeles and Huntsville, Texas. The program, dubbed "BookUp," provides urban youth with $50 a semester to spend on the books of their choice to build their own library. So far, it has successfully introduced hundreds of young people to the joys of reading. According to surveys conducted by the program, the students who participate develop more confidence, become better speakers and are more willing to share their opinions. They also develop a thirst for knowledge – defying stereotypes that by the age of nine, the average child has stopped reading for pleasure.

To the child who reads and/or becomes an author, a book is a reward for a job well done. To children who learn to "BookUp," it's a nonstop lesson on a road paved with adventure.

Make Everything About Reading

The alarm clock wails and you hit the floor running, hoping to squeeze in a bit of exercise or quiet time before dressing for the office and getting your children ready for school. While they wrestle with bed covers or complain about what they do or do not want to wear, you prepare breakfast and rustle up a few sandwiches for their lunch.

And this is just the morning ritual.

By the time evening rolls around, you're dashing from work to a dance recital or soccer practice. There might even be a little league game, cheerleading practice, an evening track meet. After all that, you must cook or pick up dinner and help at least one child with homework. Then there are those clothes that have been piling up on the laundry room floor.

With demands like these, who can think about reading? How can an overextended parent juggle library trips, book reports and other extracurricular literary activities?

The answer is simple. Adjust your family's reading to your schedule and establish methods that are less time consuming or complicated.

In other words, plant seeds. As parent, your job is to get your children to want to read. How? You make everything about reading. You talk about it over breakfast; you mention story characters while walking with your children through the mall. In fact, if you pass a bookstore, step inside. You don't have to buy anything, but you do have to make the visit seem important. If you don't have time to browse through the store, simply point to it and say something positive as you walk past with a smile.

Your goal is to promote a love of literature. Once the desire has been downloaded into their curious minds, you don't have to hover over them like whirring helicopters. It's just a matter of shifting their perspective. Think about it. Sports is a big priority because people enjoy it and because it's constantly being discussed. It's on the news, on the radio, in song lyrics, part of movies and, often, a hot topic around the house. It is deemed

> **When I say to a parent, 'read to a child,' I don't want it to sound like medicine. I want it to sound like chocolate.**
>
> – Mem Fox –

important. It generates big money and when children sign up for a team, parents – even the busy ones – like to get involved. According to a 2015 survey by the Pew Research Center, at least 37 percent of fathers have helped coach their child in a sports or athletic activity.

If sports can be glorified, then so can books. All you have to do is quietly ease it into the lives of your children in ways they don't suspect. Let's say you're planning to bake cookies for church, your child's birthday party or a family gathering. Bake them in the shape of Harry Potter characters or miniature books. Check online and you'll find plenty of websites that sell cookie cutters in the shape of Potter and other characters.

When baking a cake or pie, try a different approach. Use decorative icing to write a book title on top of the dessert. You can do the same thing with the sauce you pour over the meatloaf or the cheese coating on a spaghetti dinner. Shape the cheese slices into popular children's book titles: *Bud, Not Buddy* or *The People Could Fly* or *Diary of a Wimpy Kid.*

Your children will get a kick out of it. They might even look forward to it or laugh about it while enjoying their meal. This might also be a good time for you to repeat a favorite line from a popular novel and ask them to guess the source. It's perfect family banter and it's a sneaky but effective way to point their minds in the right direction. Your children may not be clamoring for books just yet, but they are thinking about the very things you want them to think about – fantasy, adventure, history and more.

Here are a few more quick and easy subliminal techniques:

▩ Create placemats featuring the covers of popular children's books. Depending on the ages of your children, include picture books, easy-readers, middle grade and young adult novels. Your children can make the placemats or you can hire a local art student to make them for a price you can afford.

▩ If it's in your budget, buy glasses and dishes with images of literary characters. If they're too pricey, buy paper cups from the dollar store and ask your children to write book titles or the names of their favorite book heroes on the sides of the cups.

- Hang a reward poster on the kitchen wall. The poster should offer a reward to the first child in the family who can name the characters of five books over dinner. The reward doesn't have to be monetary. For instance, the winning child could be awarded a week of no chores, be permitted to stay up an extra 20 minutes after bedtime or be allowed to select the dessert the family will eat that week.

- Order free or discounted magazine subscriptions in your child's name. Let's face it, children rarely receive good, old-fashioned mail. But it excites them. They'll be so delighted, they'll flip through the magazines and even read a couple of articles, especially if they pertain to their personal interests. Some free children's publications include: *LEGO Club Magazine* (published six times a year), *Kids' Guide to Helping Animals* (one free issue) and *Animal Wellness Magazine* (one free sample). Free online publications include *Kids Discover Online, National Geographic Kids* and *Sports Illustrated Kids.*

- Leave-a-book/Take-a-book boxes are everywhere these days. You probably have seen them. Often, they look like mailboxes sitting conspicuously in public parks or looming in front of public buildings. Or they might be a plain box in the corner of a store in your neighborhood. You and your child can drop a book in the box and take the book of your choice, or you can simply take a book without dropping off anything. The key word is free. And, you get to keep it.

- When you go to the grocery store, ask the younger children to read the backs of boxes of cereal and share what they learned.

- Buy every family member a journal and ask them to keep weekly notes of their feelings, experiences and wishes. The journal does not need to be pricey. You can find nice, shiny ones for as little as a dollar. The main thing is that your children jot down their feelings now and then and develop an appreciation for the written word.

- On your way to soccer practice or basketball tryouts, ask your children to read license plates on the cars ahead of them and come up with a word for each letter. Next, tell them to create a sentence with those words or the title of a story. No, this isn't the same thing as reading a book. But, it's the first step. It can stir up curiosity and make the art of reading seem more inviting and less intimidating.

Few things in life are more pleasurable than reading.

- Laura Vanderkam -

Laura Vanderkam, author of several time management and productivity books, including *168 Hours: You Have More Time Than You Think* (Portfolio, 2010), put it this way: "Few things in life are more pleasurable than reading." On a scale of one to ten, Vanderkam states that when people actually set aside time to read a good book, that experience ranks 8.3 – higher than movies or TV. Not everyone associates reading with bliss, she says, because they haven't given it a chance. Vanderkam blames the misunderstanding on organization and time management. If more people knew how to work books into their schedule, Vanderkam is confident that attitudes about them would change.

"Even the busiest people have leisure time," said Vanderkam. "The difference between readers and nonreaders is that readers make a habit of picking up books during fallow times."

Anne Bogel, who runs the women's lifestyle blog, *Modern Mrs. Darcy*, is another example. Although she works a part-time second job and homeschools her four children, she reads about a dozen books a month. She just builds it into her schedule. "I have certain times that I almost always read: half an hour before bed, half an hour while the kids are supposed to be in daily rest time." She also reports that, "I read in the pockets of time that other people use to check their phones and their email, again." She'll read while waiting for food to heat up in the microwave. Even if that's just five minutes a day, that buys you 35 minutes of extra reading time per week. Bogel also listens to audiobooks while she exercises. "At first, I thought I'd be happier listening to something peppier like music while I run, but then I started getting through two extra books a month…and changed my mind."

Consider every minute and every situation an opportunity to cram in another chapter, article or blurb. That means doctor's offices, grocery store lines, hair salons, barber shops and even gas stations – places where you and your children often find yourselves waiting around and staring at blank walls. Be proactive. Make sure everyone in the family always has a paperback novel, a digest of crossroad puzzles or magazine handy. It's a good way to fill in those long, boring gaps that make you yawn.

The Land of Triumph

Congratulations. You have now wired your child's brain for reading. It's part of them now. They have moved beyond their aversion to books and, in fact, have begun to crave them. What's next?

High expectations. Just like Master Caleb, the four-year-old quoted on the right, your young readers will be enthralled with their newfound hobby. To top it off, they might embark on a quest for trivia, fun facts, anything to feed that voracious book appetite. They'll want to know where bumblebees go during the winter, why birds sing and if ants really fight wars. Your little bookworms might bombard you with worldly questions you can't answer or hit you with facts you've never heard. Her mind is searching. His thoughts are maturing. Suddenly, your children are competing in spelling bees, excelling in English classes or signing up for the debate team. They might be yearning to travel to exotic places, study Mandarin or enroll in a summer school class that focuses only on the Tyrannosaurus Rex. (No doubt, the class doesn't exist, but it won't stop them from asking.)

Simply listen and guide them in the right direction. If that direction is easily accessible, do it. If it's something out of your reach – quantum physics or an expensive space camp – check with a counselor at school to make sure they stay on track and receive all the support they need.

It's not unusual for avid readers to fantasize. Don't be alarmed. Could be, their minds are expanding and they are becoming critical thinkers. Your son or daughter could be on the way to becoming a lawyer, journalist, author or politician. The important thing is that you continue to nurture their interests and allow them to grow.

How? Here's a list of do's and don'ts.

DON'TS

- Do not tell them to stop asking you so many questions.
- Do not suggest that any question is stupid.
- Do not challenge the information they share. If your child makes a statement that is incorrect, simply ask him or her where they derived the information. Together, the two of you can explore and come up with the right answer. This is a good way to build self-confidence and encourage his newfound passion for learning.

> **I read. That's my superpower... I personally read every day and absolutely love the adventure of reading.**
> - Master Caleb Stewart -
> A four-year-old motivational speaker

■ Do not limit access to the library. Taking away a favorite book is a no-no. Never punish a child by placing a limitation on reading.

DO'S

- Do continue to collect books, no matter how large the home library has become.
- Do give books as presents.
- Do fan the flames of reading.
- Do continue to read as a family.
- Do request occasional book reports.
- Do continue the book hand-me-down cycle. As one child moves to a higher grade, he or she should pass on books to younger brothers and sisters.

That's it! Your children are now gurus of the written word, which means they have made it all the way to third base. But they still have to slide into home plate. So, don't get overconfident about their success and rest on your laurels too soon.

Keep the reading nights going and continue conjuring up clever ways to fuel their budding interests. Reading expos are still as important now as they were when you were trying to entice them to pry open a book. However, now you can take it up a few notches.

Instead of limiting the family to children's book festivals, you can plan a vacation to New York and take everyone to a national reading event that caters to all ages. If New York doesn't fit your budget or your schedule, check with your local library. Fairs that focus on books are as common as sporting events. As your children become more and more curious about the world, they will regard book fairs for what they are – multifaceted events that offer crafts, meetings with authors and superheroes, games, prizes, rock-wall climbing and a range of other activities.

They'll be so eager to participate, you won't have to plead. They will be on a pilgrimage. Starry-eyed and determined, they will morph into eager travelers, learners, curiosity-seekers. Their hearts will be on fire and their brains will demand to be fed constantly. At this point, you'll have only one job: Make sure they never run out of literature.

It's their soul food – and their primary pathway into *The Wonder of Words*.

Afterword

Please don't take what you have just read lightly. I presented some of it in a humorous manner and I used as many fun exercises, anecdotes and activities as I could. However, that does not mean my sole intent is to amuse the reader. On the contrary, this book was written to inspire.

True, I tried very hard to downplay the daunting aspects of reading. But that was merely a ploy I used to make a point. I want students and parents alike to view the reading experience as more than a humdrum habit of browsing the evening newspaper or that dreaded memory we all have of being forced to read a boring book at school.

To accomplish my goal, I overemphasized the hilarity of reading. That was my way of proving that reading does not have to be dull. It doesn't have to be limited to scholars. It isn't something you do as a last resort. Reading is a means to an end and a luxurious mental process. It can be part of your daily regimen – an easy way to exercise the brain, seek out knowledge and gain a better grasp on the complexities of life.

It's also a wonderful form of self-expression. Not everyone is drawn to the same type of literature. People are no more prone to read the same publications than they are to watch the same movie or listen to the same music. Reading tastes are as individual as tastes in clothing, jokes, hobbies and leisurely pastimes.

This book was written to promote that idea and introduce methods for stimulating the literary appetite. Every chapter presented the practice of reading as an action, a force, an active verb. Every chapter showed how reading can stir up the soul, ignite interests and wake up lazy, sleepy minds.

In my opinion, this task isn't just important. It is critical. Our future depends upon it. Without it, what would happen to libraries, bookstores and magazines? Who would direct our children to a greater understanding of history, their imagination or foreign affairs?

I shudder to think that our planet would sink into the kind of dystopia author Ray Bradbury created in his acclaimed novel, *Fahrenheit 451*. The title is based on the temperature at which paper burns because that's exactly what happens in the apocalyptic world envisioned by Bradbury. In *Fahrenheit 451*, books are nonexistent. Technology rules and punishment is meted out to anyone who possesses or is seen flipping through the pages of a book. Whenever reading materials are discovered, they are confiscated and burned.

At the risk of sounding pessimistic, the exaggerated scenario I just described is one of my worst fears. I believe our children absolutely must grow up in a climate that promotes intellectual pursuits and applauds those who endeavor to ponder, write and pontificate.

The Wonder of Words represents my effort to keep these ideals alive. I'm closing it with a comprehensive reading list that will assist parents in finding books that are the right fit for their family. Remember, they all will not have the same interests and sometimes the comment, "I don't like to read," simply means they are rejecting what's been placed before them so far.

As I suggested in previous comments, this is a journey and you must guide your children through it if you want them to grow. The next several pages are packed with intriguing book titles – from the clever but silly antics of mischief makers to the heroic efforts of boxing champions, war veterans and Olympic athletes.

Peruse the list with the understanding that the brilliance of tomorrow is promised to those who recognize that past and present events are better than diamonds. They serve as sparkling fodder for authors who reimagine them, stretch them, breathe in new life, then present them back to us in the lovely form of a book.

Happy Reading!

Curtis L. Ivery

Recommended Reading

Consider this interesting hypothesis: Studies from the University of Washington and other academic institutions reveal that our personalities are formed by age 7. That means well before we reach our teens, most humans are already little grown-ups, demonstrating much of the behavior we will take into adulthood. As you search for books, keep in mind that you are helping to shape that behavior, as well as hone interests. More than any other medium, books offer facts, details, insights and theories that movies, television shows and other media simply can't deliver in equal measure. What's more, researchers have discovered that reading helps guard against loneliness. Turns out books are more than just a collection of pages; they're friends that help ensure your kids grow into informed, secure, self-assured adults. This list – intended to help navigate that process – is an age-specific glossary of early readers, cherished classics, motivational guides, humorous tales and modern masterpieces. Enjoy!

AGES 3-7

The Wonderful Things You Will Be
By Emily Winfield Martin

Goodnight Moon
By Margaret Wise Brown

Ada Twist, Scientist
By Andrea Beaty

What If You Had T. Rex Teeth?
And Other Dinosaur Parts.
By Sandra Markle

Clifford the Big Red Dog
By Norman Bridwell

The Stinky Cheese Man and Other Fairly Stupid Tales
By Jon Scieszka and Lane Smith

Cloudy with a Chance of Meatballs
By Judi Barrett and Ronald Barrett

Jabari Jumps
By Gaia Cornwall

The Story of Ferdinand
By Munro Leaf

Horton Hears a Who!
By Dr. Seuss

Recommended Reading cont

AGES 8-10

**Harry Potter and the Philosopher's Stone
(Harry Potter series, #1)**
By J.K. Rowling

**How to Train Your Dragon
(How to Train Your Dragon, #1)**
By Cressida Cowell

Woof!
By Allan Ahlberg

The Chocolate Touch
By Patrick Skene Catling

The Crossover (Crossover series, #1)
By Kwame Alexander

**The Tale of Despereaux: Being the Story of a Mouse,
a Princess, Some Soup, and a Spool of Thread**
By Kate DiCamillo

**Whoosh!: Lonnie Johnson's Super-Soaking
Stream of Inventions**
By Chris Barton

Diary of a Wimpy Kid
By Jeff Kinney

The Iron Giant
By Ted Hughes

**The Adventures of Captain Underpants
(Captain Underpants series, #1)**
By Dav Pilkey

AGES 10-13

Goosebumps: Welcome to Dead House (Goosebumps, #1)
By R.L. Stine

A Wrinkle in Time (the graphic novel)
By Madeleine L'Engle

Hip-Hop High School
By Alan Lawrence Sitomer

The Red Pyramid (The Kane Chronicles, #1)
By Rick Riordan

Bad Island
By Doug TenNapel

The Wild Robot
By Peter Brown

**The Lightning Thief
(Percy Jackson and the Olympians, #1)**
By Rick Riordan

The Carpet People
By Terry Pratchett

Sidekicks
By Dan Santat

Maniac Magee
By Jerry Spinelli

AGES 13-17

The Hunger Games (The Hunger Games, #1)
By Suzanne Collins

Perfect Chemistry (Perfect Chemistry, #1)
By Simone Elkeles

Ichiro
By Ryan Inzana

The Curious Incident of the Dog in the Night-Time
By Mark Haddon

Amy and Roger's Epic Detour
By Morgan Matson

Miles Morales: Spider Man (a graphic novel)
By Jason Reynolds

Shiver (Wolves of Mercy Falls, #1)
By Maggie Stiefvater

Flipped
By Wendelin Van Draanen

Eleanor & Park
By Rainbow Rowell

**The Summer I Turned Pretty
(The Summer I Turned Pretty, #1)**
By Jenny Han

Books ABOUT CHILDREN OF COLOR

The Colorful Adventures of Cody & Jay, A Coloring and Activity Book (ages 3 to 6)
By Crystal Swain Bates

Bippity Bop Barbershop (ages 3 to 6)
By Natasha Tarpley

Keena Ford and The Secret Journal Mix-up (ages 5 to 7)
By Melissa Thomson.

The Colored Car (ages 9 to 13)
By Jean Alicia Elster

Benny and the Basketball Bully (7 to 9)
By David Watkins

Papa, Take My Hand (a series) (ages 8 to 12)
By Angela Ivery & Curtis L. Ivery

Daphne Definitely Doesn't Do Drama (ages 10 to 14)
By Tami Charles.

Recommended Reading cont

Books ABOUT CHILDREN OF COLOR cont

**Clubhouse Mysteries Super Sleuth Collection
(ages 9 to 13)**
By Sharon M. Draper.

Ghost Boys (ages 9 to 12)
By Jewell Parker Rhodes

Black Cowboy, Wild Horses (ages 9 to 12)
By Julius Lester & Jerry Pinkney

President of the Whole Fifth Grade (ages 9 to 11)
By Sherri Winston

Dear Primo: A Letter to my Cousin (ages 8 to 11)
By Duncan Tonatiuh

Mango, Abuela, and Me (ages 8 to 11)
By Meg Medina

The Watsons Go To Birmingham (ages 9 to 13)
By Christopher Paul Curtis

One Crazy Summer (ages 9 to 13)
By Rita Williams-Garcia

The Cheetah Girls (a series) (ages 10 to 14)
By Deborah Gregory

**Marisol McDonald Doesn't Match;
Marisol McDonald No Combina (ages 8 to 10)**
By Monica Brown

Junebug (ages 8 to 11)
By Alice Mead

INSPIRATIONAL BOOKS

AGES 5-8

No Mirrors In My Nana's House
By Ysaye M. Barnwell

Salt in His Shoes
By Deloris Jordan

Dancing with the Sun
By Suzanne Marshall

Dear Little Black Boy, You Are Important and Loved
By Miss Trish

ABC: What Can She Be
By Sugar Snap Studio and Jessie Ford

I Love My Hair
By Natasha Anastasia Tarpley

I Am (Positive Affirmations for Brown Boys)
By Ayesha Rodriguez

Sparkly Me
By Ally Nathaniel

Emi's Curly, Coily, Cotton Candy Hair
By Tina Olajide

Summer Jackson: Grown Up
By Teresa E. Harris

AGES 8-12

**You Are A Unicorn:
The Fun Creative Journal For Everyone**
By Vincent Vincent

The Boy Who Never Gave Up
By Stephen Curry

Girls Rule
By Ashley Rice

**Lebron James' The Children's Book:
From a Boy to the King of Basketball**
By John Emerson

**Amelia Spreads Love Wherever She Goes:
Books About Bullying & Girl Empowerment**
By Suzanne Marshall

AGES 13 AND UP

Loving Me, Blocking Him
By Michelle Parizon

Letters to a Young Brother
By Hill Harper

Letters to a Young Sister
By Hill Harper

**Don't Give Up, Don't Give In:
Wisdom and Strength for Young Black Men**
By Curtis L. Ivery

Girl in the Mirror, A Teen's Guide to Self Awareness
By Denise Crittendon

**Life is a Party that Comes with Exams
(A Youth Empowerment Guide)**
By Denise Crittendon

**We Beat the Street
(The Three Doctors)**
By Drs. George Jenkins, Rameck Hunt and Sampson Davis

Don't Sweat the Small Stuff for Teens
By Richard Carlson

REVIEWS

So you say your book dragons are leaping hurdles and eagerly devouring book after book? Here's a breakdown of a few classics and contemporary page turners that will either challenge them, quench their thirst for knowledge or make them laugh out loud.

Ages 3-7

Ada Twist, Scientist
By Andrea Beaty. Illustrated by David Roberts

Wherein a curious young African-American girl learns the beauty of problem solving through scientific experimentation. Inspired by the true-life sagas of pioneering female computer scientist Ada Lovelace and Nobel Prize-winning chemist Marie Curie.

Zen Shorts
Written and illustrated by Jon J. Muth

Inspired by Buddhist philosophy, this engaging book tells the story of a giant panda who teaches three kids about materialism, morality and patience. Author Jon. J. Muth is himself an inspiration, supplying both the book's imaginative prose and dazzling watercolor illustrations.

The Magic Tree House (a series)
Written by Mary Pope Osborne, Illustrated by Sal Murdocca

A mystical tree house transports heroes Jack and Annie through a whirlwind of adventures, including a hurricane, an Egyptian tomb and a romp in space. This is the perfect book for curious children who are yearning to travel and learn more about the world around them.

The Wonderful Things You Will Be
By Emily Winfield Martin

Combining delightful poetry and richly rendered illustrations, author Emily Winfield Martin has created the perfect book for parents wondering what their children will become. Imbued with a sweet sense of curiosity, you'll enjoy this book as much, if not more, than your kids.

I Hate School
By Jeanne Willis and Tony Ross

Many kids will relate to this book, the saga of a girl who finds school so tormenting, she imagines that her classmates are pirates and that the cafeteria staff is feeding her worms. After finally graduating, she misses the larger-than-life characters she once complained about. A lightly grumpy book for kids adjusting to school and socialization.

Listening with My Heart:
A Story of Kindness and Self-Compassion
By Gabi Garcia. Illustrated by Ying Hui Tan

Our heroine, Esperanza, discovers a heart-shaped rock that inspires her to be more generous and forgiving. But when she experiences a crushing personal failure, Esperanza is challenged to be more generous and forgiving to herself. Readers will tap the lessons in self-compassion contained here throughout their lives.

Those Shoes
By Maribeth Boelts. Illustrated by Noah Z. Jones

A modern parable with sole. Jeremy desperately wants the flashy, expensive shoes all the cool kids have, but the family budget only allows for the essentials. Jeremy's envy and desire lead him on a journey that teaches him the value of simplicity. Parents will love this teachable fable for our consumerist culture.

The Giving Tree
By Shel Silverstein

Published in 1964, this modern classic relates the tale of a tree that provides shade and a playground for a boy, and lumber for a house and a boat in his adult years. Use this acclaimed and controversial book to prompt family discussions about nature, unconditional love, gratitude and paying it forward.

Wabi Sabi
By Mark Reibstein. Illustrated by Ed Young

Gorgeously illustrated, *Wabi Sabi* spins the tale of a Japanese cat who contemplates the origins of her curious name. Using simple haiku poetry, author Mark Reibstein acquaints young readers with the Japanese philosophy of wabi sabi, which gently teaches acceptance of change and imperfection.

The Story of Ferdinand
By Munro Leaf

Strong and muscular, the Spanish bull named Ferdinand seems perfectly suited for bullfighting. But unlike his combat-trained peers, Ferdinand enjoys sitting under trees, smelling flowers and otherwise savoring nature. This 1936 book is a classic whose message of self-love is no bull.

Ages 8-10

Who Was (a series)

Informative and entertaining, this Penguin Workshop series features editions dedicated to legendary historical figures, including Leonardo da Vinci, Abraham Lincoln, Harriet Tubman, Sacagawea, Albert Einstein, Jackie Robinson, Barack Obama, Sonya Sotomayor, and dozens more. The series' ethnic scope is breathtaking, covering the real-life sagas of folkloric heroes from Europe, Africa, Asia, Latin America and North America. Color this series "essential."

In the Year of the Boar and Jackie Robinson
By Bette Boa Lord. Illustrated by Marc Simont

Author Bette Boa Lord hits a home run in this book about Shirley Temple Wong, a Chinese immigrant whose family settles in postwar Brooklyn, N.Y. A stranger in a strange land, Shirley assimilates to American culture by following the feats of black Major League Baseball pioneer Jackie Robinson.

How to Train Your Dragon (a series)
By Cressida Cowell

What better way to feed your child's Book Dragon than a book about a dragon? This classic, multi-volume series follows the exploits of Hiccup Horrendous Haddock III, a young Norseman determined to become a hero. His first adventure – capture and train a dragon! In all, a book that's imaginative, high energy and fire-breathing funny.

Charlotte's Web
By E.B. White

This poignant 1952 tale of a timid pig who befriends a motherly spider inspires with its lessons about humanity, loss and hope. A boomer classic that still drives young readers hog wild.

Whoosh!:
Lonnie Johnson's Super-Soaking Stream of Inventions
By Chris Barton

The fascinating, real-life story of NASA engineer Lonnie Johnson, a curious African-American tinkerer who invents the Super Soaker, the glorified water pistol ranked as one of the best-selling toys of all time. Through Johnson's many initial failures, readers learn the importance of experimentation and perseverance.

Millions
By Frank Cottrell Boyce

Two siblings discover a sack full of money, only to learn the cash will lose its value within days. Their initial excitement yields to confusion as the brothers come to learn they no longer can discern the true worth of anything. Savvy parents will use this fast-paced romp as a springboard for discussions about the pursuit of happiness.

The People Could Fly: American Black Folktales
By Virginia Hamilton. Illustrated by Leo & Diane Dillon, Ph.D.

Author Virginia Hamilton serves up 24 African-American folk tales, written in a modern voice that blows the dust off black folklore. The accompanying artwork by illustrators Leo and Diane Dillon bring these centuries-old tales to vivid life.

Harry Potter (a series)
By J.K. Rowling

The best-selling sword 'n' sorcery saga for the post-boomer generation, the Harry Potter series engages young readers with its briskly paced tales of young Harry Potter, a student wizard who engages in battle with arch nemesis, Lord Voldemort. The series – including the volumes *The Philosopher's Stone*, *The Goblet of Fire*, and more – is sure to bring out the wizard in your child.

The Crossover (a series)
By Kwame Alexander

For the budding sports lover in your family, this series employs rapid-fire rhyme to convey the excitement of basketball and soccer. Including the titles *Rebound, Booked* and *The Crossover*, author Kwame Alexander has created a series that echoes the streetwise, rat-a-tat rhythms of hip hop music. Score!

A is for Activist
By Innosanto Nagara

An alphabet book of a delectably different sort. As its title attests, *A is for Activist* teaches the alphabet while advocating for social justice. Sample entry: "A is for Activist./Advocate. Abolitionist. Ally./Actively Answering A call to Action." By the time you and your kids are finished, you'll be giving author Innosanto Nagara an "A" for good intentions.

Ages 10-13

Who Am I Without Him?: Short Stories About Girls and the Boys in Their Lives
By Sharon G. Flake

With its spot-on depictions of girls approaching womanhood, *Who Am I Without Him?* triumphantly presents some of the challenges young females face as they seek to reconcile their individuality against social pressures to appease men. Coming-of-age stories shot through with warm realism.

The Carpet People
By Terry Pratchett

In this wall-to-wall romp of a book, author Terry Pratchett spins the story of the Munrungs, a Lilliputian-like species that lurks deep in the piles of carpets. Adventure ensues when a mysterious force called "Fray" disrupts the Munrungs' placid world. A wonderful and thought-provoking meditation on cultures and change.

Number the Stars
By Lois Lowry

Set in wartime Denmark, *Number the Stars* details both the horrors and acts of bravery that marked World War II. It's the story of Annemarie Johansen, whose family adopts Annemarie's best friend, Ellen Rosen, as their own, concealing her Jewish lineage from Nazi troops. In vibrant text, author Lowry reveals how the Danish Resistance smuggled nearly all of Denmark's Jewish population to the safety of Sweden's shores. Inspiring.

I Am Not Your Perfect Mexican Daughter
By Erika L. Sanchez

In this bold yet humorous story, a Mexican girl named Julia grows up in the shadow of her accomplished sister, Olga. When Olga dies suddenly, Julia slowly discovers that her sister wasn't nearly as perfect as everyone believed. A book that delivers powerful lessons about living up to other folks' expectations.

Diary of a Wimpy Kid (a series)
By Jeff Kinney

A sort of graphic novel for the preteen set, this popular book series follows the exploits of student Greg Heffley as he drolly journals his humdrum middle school existence. Author Jeff Kinney writes in pitch-perfect preteen tones, capturing all the eye-rolling world weariness of a nerdy kid far too young to be world weary.

Monster
By Walter Dean Myers

A book that will satisfy your adolescent's appetite for keep-it-real drama. In this NY Times best-seller, author Walter Dean Myers tells the story of Steve Harmon, a teen in juvenile detention awaiting trial. The book illustrates how one person's bad decisions can alter the course of many lives.

Percy Jackson and the Olympians (a series)
By Rick Riordan

Over 45 million readers can't be wrong. This series will catapult your kids into the awe-inspiring world of classical Greek mythology, with its enthralling cast of characters including Zeus, Achilles, Poseidon, Athena, and more. Start at the first volume, *The Lightning Thief,* and follow Percy through five book volumes and numerous related works.

A Wrinkle in Time
By Madeleine L'Engle

Bedeviled by rumors that their father abandoned their scientist mother, siblings Meg and Charles Wallace embark on a journey through time to find their father. Their search forces them to confront a mystical force that is darkening the galaxies. An empowering saga for kids on the cusp of adolescence.

Hip-Hop High School
By Alan Sitomer

When young Theresa Anderson finds herself pigeonholed as the street-wise black sheep to her overachieving brother, she seeks comfort in rap music, with its endless array of rebellious misfits. Everything changes when Theresa meets Devon, an around-the-way boy whose gangsta image conceals contradictory academic ambitions. An intriguingly coiled plot showcasing an emotionally complex heroine for our pop culture times.

Maniac Magee
By Jerry Spinelli

Issues of racism, illiteracy and homelessness gracefully intersect in Jerry Spinelli's book about Jeffrey Lionel "Maniac" Magee, an orphan living with his tightly wound aunt and uncle. When Jeffrey discovers running, he is transformed into Maniac Magee, a local legend who alters his racially divided town. An adolescent anthem to self-realization.

Ages 13-17

I Am Malala
By Malala Yousafzai

The youngest Nobel Peacc Prize winner in history, author Malala Yousafzai was thrust into the global spotlight after terrorists brutally attacked her for advocating education for girls in her native Pakistan. In this moving 2013 memoir – written at the tender age of 16 – Yousafzai recounts her struggle while hailing the efforts of kindred human rights advocates. A powerful portrait in courage that will inspire readers for life.

My Side of the Mountain
By Jean Craighead George

First published in 1959, this classic is, ultimately, a meditation on the dualistic beauty and dangers of the material world and human nature. A troubled New York City kid named Sam Gribley runs off into the mountains where he discovers himself through a series of encounters with the natural world and its animal inhabitants. Thought provoking and richly detailed.

Ichiro
By Ryan Inzana

Beautifully written and handsomely illustrated, *Ichiro* is the story of an Asian-American boy who moves to Japan to live with his mother's family. Through his grandfather, "Ichi" learns about ancient Japanese mythology, prompting the boy to contemplate the complexities of spirituality, war and human conflict.

The Curious Incident of the Dog in the Night-Time
By Mark Haddon

A murder mystery with a contemporary twist. When 15-year-old Christopher Boone discovers a neighborhood dog dead on his family's lawn, the shocking sight sends the boy on an investigation to determine the cause of death. Author Mark Haddon demonstrates deft storytelling skill in this thoroughly absorbing tale.

Roots: The Saga of an American Family

By Alex Haley

The slave saga that launched a history-making TV miniseries. *Roots* finds author Alex Haley tracing his lineage back to his great-great-great-grandfather, a West African named Kunta Kinte, who was captured and brought to the US in 1750. Spanning two centuries, Haley's exhaustive research and storytelling prowess brings his family to life. In all, *Roots* is the story of the United States, in all its racially divided complexity.

The Summer I Turned Pretty (a trilogy)

By Jenny Han

As its curious title suggests, *The Summer I Turned Pretty* is a coming-of-age story about a teen-aged girl's sexual awakening. For years, Isabel "Belly" Conklin has carried a torch for hunk and family friend, Conrad Fischer. Finally, one summer, she discovers that Conrad shares her infatuation – as does Conrad's brother, Jeremiah. Including the volumes *It's Not Summer Without You* and *We'll Always Have Summer,* this trilogy is a page-turner for the Millennial set.

Flipped

By Wendelin Van Draanen

This 2003 romantic teen comedy is a classic for good reason. The book captures with pinpoint accuracy the constantly shifting dynamics of romance. Since second grade, Julianna "Juli" Baker has had a thing for classmate Bryce Loski, but Bryce repeatedly rebuffs her overtures. Author Wendelin Van Draanen chronicles the pair's constant miscues with exemplary comic flair.

Out of Darkness

By Ashley Hope Pérez

This book may be set in 1930s Texas, but *Out of Darkness* reveals that issues of interracial love and forbidden romance are nothing new. Naomi, a 15-year-old Mexican girl, arrives in San Antonio with her younger biracial half-siblings. Her intensifying crush on an African-American boy forces her to negotiate the volatility of a racially divided town.

Persepolis (two volumes)

By Marjane Satrapi

A graphic autobiography that helps demystify Iran and the Middle East, P*ersepolis* – and its companion volume *Persepolis 2* – depicts the childhood of author Marjane Satrapi in bold narrative strokes. Ably juggling detail, insight and dark humor, volume one recounts Satrapi's upbringing during the Islamic Revolution, while *Persepolis 2* details the author's high school years in Austria.

Flour Babies

By Anne Fine

You might expect a teen-centric story about childrearing to have a female protagonist, but *Flour Babies* tells the story of Martin Simon, an underprivileged 14-year-old assigned by his school teacher to spend three weeks nurturing a surrogate "baby" made from a bag of flour. The assignment leads Simon on a series of self-discoveries that help him come to terms with his own absentee dad.

BIOGRAPHIES

Who Was Neil Armstrong?
By Roberta Edwards

Brown Girl Dreaming
By Jacqueline Woodson

I Dissent: Ruth Bader Ginsburg Makes Her Mark
By Debbie Levy and Elizabeth Baddeley

Malcolm Little: The Boy Who Grew Up to Become Malcolm X
By Ilyasah Shabazz

Little Leaders
By Vashti Harrison

Who is Michelle Obama?
By Megan Stine

Martin's Big Words, the Life of Dr. Martin Luther King, Jr. (young readers)
By Doreen Rappaport

You Should Meet Mae Jemison (Ready to Read)
By Laurie Calkhoven

Ghost Boys (Emmet Till and other historical figures)
By Jewell Parker Rhodes

SPECIALTY BOOKS

HAVING FUN WITH MATH

The Dot & the Line
By Norton Juster

Anno's Mysterious Multiplying Jar
By Masaichiro and Mitsumasa Anno

Pattern Fish
By Trudy Harris

Sir Cumference and the Dragon of Pi
By Cindy Neuschwander

12 Ways to Get to 11
By Eve Merriam

The Grapes of Math
By Greg Tang

SCIENCE (for fourth graders)

The Tree of Life: The Incredible Biodiversity of Life on Earth
By Rochelle Strauss

This book leads children of all ages on an exploration of life forms including fish, birds, reptiles, amphibians and mammals.

Wild Animals of North America
By the National Geographic Society

From owls to bison, elementary school students are introduced to a wide range of wildlife.

Who Pooped in the Park? Grand Canyon National Park: Scat and Tracks for Kids
By Gary D. Robson

Two children and their parents learn to track animals via footprints and other clues to their identity.

Forces Make Things Move
By Kimberly Brubaker Bradley

Using fun, humor and an engaging tone, this book introduce Kindergarteners to basic scientific principles.

FOR DYSLEXIC READERS

My Name is Brain Brian (For boys ages 10 and older)
By Jeanne Betancourt

Dyslexia Wonders
By Jennifer Smith

Written by a 12-year-old dyslexic girl who reveals the ups and downs of her daily struggles.

Percy Jackson and the Lightning Thief
By Rick Riordan

A 12-year-old hypertensive, dyslexic boy, who is repeatedly kicked out of school, discovers he has supernatural powers.

Pony Pals Series
By Jeanne Betancourt

Three dyslexic girls have a series of escapades while riding backyard ponies. (For girls ages 10 and up)

Here's Hank Series
By Henry Winkler

Books in this series are written in a dyslexic font.

HOLIDAY BOOKS

The Best Christmas Pageant Ever
By Barbara Robinson

On the Night You Were Born
By Nancy Tillman

Polar Express
By Chris Van Allsburg

Christmas Jokes for Kids
By Aunt Lily

It's Kwanzaa Time!
The seven principles of Kwanzaa with artwork, songs, recipes and games
By Linda & Clay Goss

A Kwanzaa Celebration Pop-Up Book
By Nancy Williams and paper engineer, Robert Sabuda

Santa's Kwanzaa
By Garen Eileen Thomas

The Night Before Christmas: An African American Retelling
By Noland Nixon

The Power of Light: Eight Stories for Hanukkah
By Isaac Bashevis Singer

Hanukkah Bear
By Eric A. Kimmel

The Girl Who Saved Christmas
By Matt Haig

The Boy Who Hated Christmas
By Miriam Madison

EASTER

Easter Spot the Differences (Dover Little Activity Books)
By Becky Radtke

The Berenstain Bears and The Easter Story: Stickers included
By Jan & Mike Berenstain

It's Not Easy Being a Bunny (easy reader)
By Marilyn Sadler

Captain Awesome and the Easter Egg Bandit
By Stan Kirby

The Easter Story for Children
By Max Lucado

There Was an Old Lady Who Swallowed a Chick!
By Lucille Colandro

My Easter (multiculturalism and spirituality)
By Jennifer Blizin Gillis

ATTENTION GRABBERS and SEMI-SCARY BOOKS

Spooky stories are sure to be big hits. Why? Children love being captivated and lured to the edge of their seats. That explains the popularity of the beloved yet creepy "Goosebumps" series by R. L. Stine. But the "Goosebumps" tales, though an all-time favorite, aren't the only thrillers that send shivers down young spines. From elementary school through middle and high school, most students will gladly flip through the pages of nearly every book on this Halloween list.

Skeleton Hiccups (easy reader)
By Margery Cuyler

Room on the Broom
By Julia Donaldson

Halloween Hustle
By Charlotte Gunnufson

How to Scare a Ghost
By Jean Reagan

Here's Hank: There's a Zombie in My Bathtub *(in dyslexic font)*
By Henry Winkler

Nate the Great and the Monster Mess
By Marjorie Weinman Sharmat

MULTICULTURAL HALLOWEEN BOOKS

The Very Helpful Monsters (easy reader)
By Sally Huss

Vampire Girl
By Lenny Lee

Rise of the Jumbies (Caribbean folklore)
By Tracey Baptiste

The Adventures of Old School Brown
By Paul Edward Davis

FOR TEENS

Akata Witch
By Nnedi Okorafor

The Witch of Blackbird Pond
By Elizabeth George Speare

6 Scary Halloween Stories for Teens 2 Urban Legends
By PW Pretorius and Len du Randt

A Babysitter's Guide to Monster Hunting
By Joe Ballarini

Teenage Christian at Halloween
By Brenda Bone

Resources for Parents

Plant A Seed…Read, 101 Activities to Motivate Children to Read
By Gwendolyn R. Lewis

Fun on the Run for Kids
By Cynthia L. Copeland

NurtureShock: New Thinking About Children
By Po Bronson and Ashley Merryman

Smart Parenting for Smart Kids: Nurturing Your Child's True Potential
By Eileen Kennedy Moore & Mark S. Lowenthal

ReadingRockets.org/audience/parents

ScholasticforParents.com/parents

Jumpstart.com

www.pta.org/home/family-resources/ Parents-Guides-to-Student-Success

Facebook Group: Parents, Find Children's Books and Authors Here

Family Reading Journal

Books Your Family Has Read

1. _____
2. _____
3. _____
4. _____
5. _____
6. _____
7. _____
8. _____
9. _____
10. _____

Books Your Family Plans To Read

1. _____
2. _____
3. _____
4. _____
5. _____
6. _____
7. _____
8. _____
9. _____
10. _____

Reading Activities

Library Book Due Dates

1. _____
2. _____
3. _____
4. _____
5. _____
6. _____
7. _____
8. _____
9. _____
10. _____

Upcoming Book Fairs

1. _____
2. _____
3. _____
4. _____
5. _____
6. _____
7. _____
8. _____
9. _____
10. _____

My Favorite Books

About the Author

Curtis L. Ivery, Ph.D., a nationally renowned leader in Urban American Affairs and recipient of the 2005 Michiganian of the Year award from the *Detroit News*, was the creator and driving force behind the highly acclaimed *Educational Summit: Responding to the Crises in Urban America* and *Rebuilding Lives: Restoration, Reformation and Rehabilitation in the U.S. Criminal Justice System*, which aired on C-Span and other national television media. The author of several books and numerous newspaper and magazine articles, Ivery continues his quest to strengthen communities by rebuilding the family unit and the values that create and hold it together.

Long recognized in his efforts to bring about social change and awareness, Ivery was the first black man appointed to the Governor's Cabinet in Arkansas as the Commissioner for the Department of Health and Human Services during the 1970s. He is also an in-demand speaker for educational and civic organizations.

The son of a laborer, Ivery was taught the value of family and education, and they are the cornerstones of his personal and professional platform. Recognizing that professional success begins with the role parents play in instilling the necessary characteristics and values needed to achieve it, he has made it his personal mission to educate, inspire and actively engage African-American males in the parenting process.

Leading by example, Ivery and his wife, Ola, have not only made education and family a priority for their two adult children, Marcus and Angela, but also for children in the metropolitan Detroit area and around the United States.

Counterclockwise from upper left: Curtis L. Ivery; Ola Ivery; the Ivery's grandsons enjoy some time with their favorite books.